Zakah and Sadaqah

ZAKĀH AND ṢADAQAH

Ṣadaqah is a general term referring to anything that is done or given for the acceptance of Allāh and seeking His reward. The concept of *ṣadaqah* is wider than that of charity. The Prophet (ﷺ) said, "*Every good deed is a ṣadaqah.*"[1]

Zakāh is a specific form of *ṣadaqah*. It is an obligatory expenditure due from those Muslims who possess wealth in excess of their fundamental needs. It is among the pillars of Islām and is the right of Allāh, the Exalted, given for the benefit of the Muslim *ummah*. The word "*zakāh*" means "purification and growth." Its regular payment purifies the owner's remaining wealth and purifies his heart from such ailments as greed and selfishness.

Throughout the Makkan period the types of wealth from which *zakāh* is due were not specified nor was the quantity, contributions being left to the discretion of the owner. In the second year following the *hijrah,* the *zakāh* due from each kind of wealth was defined and clarified in detail.

OBLIGATORY ZAKĀH

Legal Status of Zakāh

Zakāh is an essential obligation according to the Qur'ān, the prophetic *sunnah* and the consensus of Muslim scholars.

+ In the Qur'ān, Allāh said:

﴿وَالَّذِينَ يَكْنِزُونَ الذَّهَبَ وَالفِضَّةَ وَلاَ يُنفِقُونَهَا فِي سَبِيلِ اللهِ فَبَشِّرهُم بِعَذَابٍ أَلِيمٍ﴾

"And those who hoard gold and silver and spend it not in the way of Allāh – give them tidings of a painful punishment."[2]

Then He ordered His Messenger (ﷺ):

﴿خُذ مِن أَموَالِهِم صَدَقَةً تُطَهِّرُهُم وَتُزَكِّيهِم بِهَا﴾

"Take from their wealth a ṣadaqah by which you purify them and cause them increase."[3]

And He ordered Muslims in general:

---

[1] Aḥmad and Muslim.
[2] *Sūrah at-Tawbah,* 9:34.
[3] *Sūrah at-Tawbah,* 9:103.

﴿وَأَقِيمُوا الصَّلَاةَ وَآتُوا الزَّكَاةَ وَأَطِيعُوا الرَّسُولَ لَعَلَّكُم تُرحَمُونَ﴾

"Establish prayer and give zakāh and obey the Messenger – that you may receive mercy."[4]

The giving of *zakāh* is mentioned in conjunction with *ṣalāh* (prayer) in twenty-six Qur'ānic verses.

♦ From the *sunnah*: When the Prophet (ﷺ) sent Mu'ādh bin Jabal to the people of Yemen, among his instructions was, "Inform them that Allāh, the Mighty and Majestic, has made incumbent upon them a *ṣadaqah* to be taken from their rich and given to their poor." And he (ﷺ) warned, "Whoever Allāh has granted wealth but does not give its *zakāh* – for him will be formed on the Day of Resurrection a poisonous snake with black growths over its eyes. It will wrap itself around his neck and then begin biting his cheeks, saying, 'I am your treasure, I am your wealth.'" Then he recited:

﴿وَلاَ يَحسَبَنَّ الَّذِينَ يَبخَلُونَ بِمَا آتَاهُمُ اللهُ مِن فَضلِه هُوَ خَيرًا لَهُم بَل هُوَ شَرٌّ لَهُم سَيُطَوَّقُونَ مَا بَخِلُوا بِه يَــومَ القِيَامَة﴾

"And let not those who withhold what Allāh has given them of His bounty ever think that it is better for them. Rather, it is worse for them. Their necks will be encircled by what they withheld on the Day of Resurrection."[5]

Being a pillar and fundamental requirement of Islām, anyone who denies the obligatory nature of *zakāh* (unless out of complete ignorance) has removed himself from the religion. One who acknowledges the obligation, although failing to fulfill it, remains a Muslim – albeit a disobedient one subject to severe punishment in the Hereafter. He is required to repent sincerely to Allāh and pay whatever he had withheld in the past.

After the death of Allāh's Messenger (ﷺ) some of the Arab tribes refused to give *zakāh,* claiming it had been due only during the Prophet's lifetime. But Abū Bakr said, "By Allāh, I will surely fight anyone who discriminates between *ṣalāh* and *zakāh.*" 'Umar and the other *ṣaḥābah* agreed that this was correct.[6]

The Intention

Zakāh is a form of worship; therefore, the *niyyah* (intention) is a condition for its validity. This means the giver must be aware that what he is giving is the obligatory *zakāh* due from him, that he seeks acceptance of it by Allāh, and that he expects reward from Him. Allāh's Messenger (ﷺ) said, "Deeds are [judged]

---

[4]*Sūrah an-Nūr,* 24:56.
[5]The Qur'ānic quote is *Sūrah Āli 'Imrān,* 3:180. Both narrations by al-Bukhārī and Muslim.
[6]Al-Bukhārī and Muslim.

only by intention."[7] The *niyyah* is knowledge and intent in the heart and is not pronounced by the tongue.

Due Date

From most kinds of excess wealth, *zakāh* is due after it has been in the owner's possession for a period of one lunar year. An exception is that for agricultural products, which is due at the time of harvest. *Zakāh* is the right of Allāh and must be given on time. It is not permissible to delay it beyond its due date unless one is prevented by circumstances beyond his control. It may, however, be given in advance when deemed beneficial, and the Prophet (ﷺ) permitted that. Overdue *zakāh,* with or without a valid excuse, is never exempted and must be calculated and paid in full, even after a lapse of many years. Anyone whose intent is to evade *zakāh* by selling, giving away or destroying property before the due date will be held accountable by Allāh.

Who Must Give Zakāh

Zakāh is due from every Muslim possessing the *niṣāb* for particular kinds of wealth. *Niṣāb* refers to the minimum amount of any type of wealth from which *zakāh is* taken. The Muslim who possesses this minimum or more must give a stipulated proportion of the entire amount as *zakāh.* The *zakāh* of a child or mentally deficient person who possesses the *niṣāb* is calculated and paid from his property by his legal guardian. It is not an obligation for a slave or a non-Muslim.

If a Muslim dies owing *zakāh,* it is paid from his estate before its distribution. In fact, it takes priority over other debts and any bequests by the deceased, for the Prophet (ﷺ) said, "The debt of Allāh has the most right to be settled."[8]

Conditions Pertaining to Wealth or Property

- ◆ The *niṣāb* must be in excess of commonly recognized basic needs such as food, clothing, living quarters, transport, the tools or instruments of one's trade, etc.

- ◆ The amount of wealth comprising the *niṣāb* should have been in the owner's possession for a complete lunar year (with the exception of agricultural produce).

- ◆ Anything saved or put aside for the payment of a debt is not included in *zakāh* calculations.

- ◆ In cases of shared ownership, the share of an individual partner must reach the *niṣāb* to be liable for *zakāh.* The total value of the shares is irrelevant.

---

[7] Al-Bukhārī and Muslim.
[8] Al-Bukhārī and Muslim.

Not every kind of wealth or property is subject to *zakāh*. The main categories stipulated in the Islāmic *sharī'ah* are:

- Gold and silver or currency representing their value
- Merchandise held for sale
- Freely grazing livestock
- Non-perishable agricultural produce

Of these, there are subdivisions, each having a specific *nisāb* and required rate for *zakāh*. None of them are combined to make a *nisāb* (for example, gold and silver or dates and raisins), but each is considered separately. Rulings are given on the following pages for those properties common in the present day.

1. Silver and Monetary Assets

Silver is inclusive of all its various forms – coins, molded objects, ore, etc., but not paint or surface plating. Paper and metal currency, bonds and the like are theoretically exchangeable for silver in most countries and are thus considered as being of the same value.

Nisāb: No *zakāh* is due on silver, cash or savings until it reaches the sum of 200 *dirhams,* or the estimated market value of 611.5 grams of silver. And nothing is due until this amount has been saved by the owner for a period of one lunar year. If it was spent during that time and then replaced, a new term would begin from the day of replacement. Income spent within the year is not subject to *zakāh* – only savings.

Rate: One fortieth (i.e., 2.5%) – The Prophet (ﷺ) said, "From two hundred *dirhams* is due one fourth of a tenth, and there is none for a hundred and ninety, unless its owner wishes."[9]

Zakāh on loans: The scholars agree that anything lent out remains a part of one's property. A loan is generally one of two kinds: that admitted by the debtor who intends and strives to pay it back, and that where the debtor is either in difficulty and continues to delay payment or denies the debt altogether.

When repayment is expected, *zakāh* is due on the loaned amount each year. The lender may either pay its due yearly from other funds in his possession or wait until the loan is repaid. In this case, he would calculate what was due from that sum during the time it was with the debtor and pay what is owed upon its receipt. There is a second opinion that no *zakāh* is due on loans, although the first is safer and more prudent.

---

[9]Al-Bukhārī.

When repayment is doubtful or not expected, no *zakāh* is due, as the lender will be unable to benefit from it. However, some scholars stipulate that upon unexpected recovery of the sum, he must pay its *zakāh* in full, while others require him to pay for that year alone.

Deferred *mahr* (the obligatory wedding gift) is a debt to the wife which she should consider as a loan. Its indefinite postponement would absolve her of its *zakāh* until the time she actually receives it.

2. Gold

Like silver, all forms of gold are included, except thin surface plating.

Niṣāb and rate: The amount for which *zakāh* is due is 20 *dīnārs,* which is equal to about 87 grams of gold. The Prophet (ﷺ) said, "When you have twenty *dīnārs* and a year has passed on them, half a *dīnār* is due."[10] Thus, the rate is also one fortieth or 2.5%, paid on the entire amount.

Jewelry: There is no *zakāh* on pearls, diamonds, sapphires or other precious stones unless they are kept for business purposes. Scholars have traditionally differed over the question of women's ornaments made from gold and silver. The two views are as follows:

- There is no *zakāh* on a woman's gold and silver jewelry. This is the view of the ash-Shāfiʿī, Mālikī and Ḥanbalī schools of thought. It is based on the opinions of some *ṣaḥābah.* Jurists who are of this view stipulate that the jewelry be worn and not stored and that it remains within the normal range for women of the owner's social standing.

- *Zakāh* is due on gold and silver jewelry once the *niṣāb* is attained. This is the view of the Ḥanafī school of thought and is based on opinions of other *ṣaḥābah* and supported by sound *ḥadīths,* among them:

- "Any owner of gold or silver who does not give its due will, on the Day of Resurrection, have it heated in the fire of Hell and made into plates with which to sear his sides, forehead and back..."[11]

- When Umm Salamah asked the Prophet (ﷺ) whether her gold anklets were considered as hoarded wealth, he said, "Whatever has been purified by giving its *zakāh* is not hoarded wealth."[12]

Additionally, it is clear that all of the *ḥadīths* mentioning *zakāh* for these two metals as well as Allāh's words **"And those who hoard gold and silver"** make no exception for jewelry or other items. Therefore, the second view is seen as stronger and preferable, especially for those who are well to do. The

---

[10] Al-Bukhārī.

[11] Aḥmad and Muslim.

[12] Abū Dāwūd – *ḥasan.*

first view may be applicable for a woman who owns little more than the gold she regularly wears, and Allāh knows best.

3. Metals and Minerals Extracted from the Earth

Ores and metals discovered in the ground without effort and expense are subject to *zakāh* immediately upon discovery, without regard to a *niṣāb* or the passing of a year. Included is treasure buried in pre-Islāmic times. The rate for such finds is 20%, paid once. Allāh's Messenger (ﷺ) said, "On buried wealth is one fifth."[13] Thereafter, the property would be subject to *zakāh* yearly if it was among the types indicated by the Prophet (ﷺ). It is agreed that such wealth discovered as a result of labor and expense is not subject to the initial one fifth.

Many scholars have ruled that anything of value extracted from the earth, such as iron, copper, precious stones, petroleum, phosphorus, etc., is liable for *zakāh* when the *niṣāb* (according to market value) has been in the owner's possession for one lunar year, on the assumption that these have commercial benefit. The rate for gold, silver and commercial commodities is 2.5%.

4. Merchandise and Commercial Commodities

The majority of scholars from the *ṣaḥābah,* the *tābi'een* and their students have ruled that *zakāh* is due on unsold merchandise one lunar year after possession when its market value reaches the *niṣāb* for silver or currency. It includes anything obtained for sale, whether real estate, machinery, equipment, clothing or any other articles, large or small. Its rate is 2.5%, as for monetary savings. The ruling is based upon the principle that commodities in stock are assets exchangeable for cash. If businessmen (generally the wealthiest members of society) could escape payment by converting their money into commodities, the purpose for which *zakāh* was ordained would be defeated. Property is considered merchandise only when two conditions are met:

- Actual possession through lawful earning, purchase, gift, bequest, etc.

- The intent at the time of acquisition that it will be for business purposes. According to one view, anything kept without that initial intent is not subject to *zakāh* for merchandise, even if the owner should decide subsequently to sell it. A second view states that it becomes merchandise when a decision is made to sell, so its *zakāh* becomes due one year from that time if still unsold.

5. Land

No *zakāh* is taken from land unless it is held explicitly for future sale. Recent *fatwās* take into account that land, like other properties in little demand, are not always saleable immediately. Owners who wait long periods for a buyer

---

[13]Al-Bukhārī and Muslim.

or a suitable market price, perhaps for years, do not benefit from its worth in the meantime. Therefore, *zakāh* is due on it only once – when it is actually sold. And Allāh knows best.

When property is leased or sold, *zakāh* is paid only on whatever income remains from the transaction after one lunar year. When leased land is cultivated, responsibility for *zakāh* falls upon the owner of the crop, not the owner of the land.

6. Rented Homes, Buildings, Automobiles and Other Possessions

There is nothing due on property acquired for renting. However, like any other income, whatever remains after one lunar year of the rent collected will be subject to *zakāh* at the rate of 2.5%.

7. Animals

Authentic *hadīths* explicitly mention the *zakāh* for camels, cattle, sheep and goats when the following conditions are present:

- Possession of the *nisāb*
- The passing on it of one lunar year
- That the livestock is freely grazing in pastures for most of the year

The narrations specify grazing animals. Those consuming feed supplied by man and whose upkeep involves expense are not of this category and are not subject to *zakāh* unless they were obtained for sale.

Niṣāb: The minimum number from which *zakāh* is taken for each is five camels, thirty heads of cattle, and forty goats or sheep. Young animals born within a herd during the year are counted as a part of the original property.

Rate:

- For each five camels under 25, one sheep or goat is due. For numbers over 25, one or more she-camels of specified ages. Further details are given in books of *fiqh*.
- For every 30 head of cattle, a one-year old. For every 40 head, a two-year old.
- For 40 to 119 sheep or goats, one. For 120 to 299, two. For 300 to 399, three. For each additional 100, one. Sheep and goats are considered as one kind and may be combined.

It is not permissible to give a defective animal in *zakāh* unless all are defective. Medium quality animals are acceptable.

Other animals or fowl raised for meat, milk, eggs, etc. are not subject to *zakāh* even when little or no expense is involved, but those obtained for sale are considered as commercial commodities.

8. Agricultural Produce

Allāh, the Exalted ordered:

﴿يَا أَيُّهَا الَّذِينَ آمَنُوا أَنفِقُوا مِن طَيِّبَاتِ مَا كَسَبْتُمْ وَمِمَّا أَخْرَجْنَا لَكُم مِّنَ الأَرْضِ﴾

"O you who have believed, spend from the good things which you have earned and from that which We have produced for you from the earth."[14]

At the time of the Prophet (ﷺ), *zakāh* was taken from four staple crops: wheat, barley, dates and raisins. There is a consensus among scholars that it is due on these four when their harvest yields the *niṣāb*. A majority also includes similar products that can be stored for periods of a year or longer, such as rice and other edible grains. There is a consensus as well that there is no *zakāh* for perishable fruits and vegetables such as cucumbers, melons and citrus fruits. Differences of opinion occur concerning that which was not specifically mentioned by the Prophet (ﷺ) or the *ṣaḥābah,* especially after the introduction of modern methods of preservation. These viewpoints may be summarized as follows:

a) *Zakāh* is due only on the four from which it was taken by the Prophet (ﷺ).

b) It is due on everything that grows in the earth, based upon the aforementioned Qur'ānic verse.

c) It is due from whatever grows in the earth on the condition that it can be kept with minimal treatment for at least a year, such as grain, seeds, cotton and sugar.

d) It is due on grain, seeds and fruits preservable by drying. Some recent *fatwā*s include what can be kept relatively long periods by refrigeration.

e) It is due on staple foods that can be stored naturally and whose seeds are planted.

The last three views are clearly based on the general objectives behind the Prophet's practice, which should be taken into account.

Due date: *Zakāh* is due on agricultural produce immediately (at the time of harvest) when it is prepared for sale, for Allāh has said:

﴿كُلُوا مِن ثَمَرِهِ إِذَا أَثْمَرَ وَآتُوا حَقَّهُ يَوْمَ حَصَادِهِ﴾

"Eat of its fruit when it yields and give its due on the day of its harvest."[15]

It is given by the owner of the crop, whether or not he owns the land.

---

[14]*Sūrah al-Baqarah,* 2:267.
[15]*Sūrah al-An'ām,* 6:141.

Niṣāb: The Prophet (ﷺ) stated, "No ṣadaqah (zakāh) is due on less than five wasqs of grain or dates."[16] This amount is approximately equal to 675 kilograms, which is far in excess of an owner's usual need and would likely be put up for sale. The niṣāb increases when the crop includes shells, husks, leaves, etc.

Rate: The percentage of zakāh differs according to how the crop is irrigated. Allāh's Messenger (ﷺ) said, "For what is watered by rain, springs or streams a tenth is due, and for what is watered by [human] irrigation half a tenth."[17] Thus, 10% is given from a harvest that was irrigated naturally without labor or expense, while only 5% is required when irrigation canals are dug and pumps or sprinklers employed. When a crop is watered partially by natural means and partially through human effort, scholars agree that the rate for zakāh becomes 7.5%.

The Muslim must give produce of good quality as zakāh, for Allāh ordered:

﴿وَلَا تَيَمَّمُوا الْخَبِيثَ مِنْهُ تُنفِقُونَ وَلَسْتُم بِآخِذِيهِ إِلَّا أَن تُغْمِضُوا فِيهِ وَاعْلَمُوا أَنَّ اللَّهَ غَنِيٌّ حَمِيدٌ﴾

"And do not aim toward the defective thereof, spending [from that] while you would not take it [yourself] except with closed eyes. And know that Allāh is Free of need and Praiseworthy."[18]

Transfer of Zakāh

From the Prophet's words "to be taken from their rich and given to their poor," it is concluded that zakāh is to be distributed primarily in the city or country where the wealth or property is located as long as there is need. However, there are circumstances that warrant its transfer to other locations, among them:

- Natural disasters, famine or health epidemics
- Lawful jihād against an enemy of Islām
- Greater poverty in other regions
- Knowledge of needy relatives in other locations
- Particular cases of urgency

Most scholars have ruled that transfer is permissible, and priorities are the responsibility of those who give and collect zakāh.

Loss of Zakāh

When zakāh is set aside for payment or distribution, the obligation is not fulfilled until it has actually been given by the owner, either to the recipient

---

[16] Al-Bukhārī and Muslim.
[17] Al-Bukhārī.
[18] Sūrah al-Baqarah, 2:267.

directly or to a distributor. Thus, if it is lost, stolen or destroyed before that, the debt remains and the owner must still give what is due, unless he no longer possesses the *niṣāb*.

Lawful Recipients of Zakāh

Those eligible for *zakāh* are of eight categories, which are stipulated in the following verse from the Qur'ān:

﴿إِنَّمَا الصَّدَقَاتُ لِلفُقَرَاءِ وَالْـــمَسَاكِينِ وَالْعَامِلِينَ عَلَيهَا وَالْــمُؤَلَّفَةِ قُلُوبُهُم وَفِي الرِّقَابِ وَالْغَارِمِينَ وَفِي سَـــبِيلِ اللهِ وَابنِ السَّبِيلِ فَرِيضَةً مِنَ اللهِ وَاللهُ عَلِيمٌ حَكِيمٌ﴾

"The ṣadaqāt [zakāh expenditures] are only for the poor, the needy, those employed for it, for uniting hearts, for freeing captives, for those in debt, for the cause of Allāh, and for the [stranded] traveler – an obligation [imposed] by Allāh. And Allāh is Knowing and Wise."[19]

Since it is not permissible to give *zakāh* to any other than these, each will be described in detail.

1. The Poor (الفقراء)

A poor man is one who does not possess *niṣāb* after covering the year's expenses for himself and his family. This is in contrast to the rich, who is self-sufficient and possesses *niṣāb* at the end of the year. The *niṣāb* for those kinds of wealth on which *zakāh* is due must be in excess of what one spends for such essential requirements as food, clothing, shelter, means of transport and equipment instrumental in earning a living or property to be rented. Anyone without some of these needs or having less than *niṣāb* after securing them is eligible to receive *zakāh*. Necessities include basic home furnishings but not such items as television sets.

2. The Needy (المساكين)

There is no difference between the poor and the needy as far as indigence is concerned, although some scholars are of the opinion that the needy are more destitute than the poor. But generally, the needy are defined as a particular type of poor – those who are too proud or too shy to ask for help, so that most people are unaware of their condition. The Prophet (ﷺ) described them thus: "The needy [*miskeen*] is not one who circulates among the people that you can satisfy with a bite or two or a date or two, but he is one who finds not means of self-sufficiency, while no one is aware to give him *ṣadaqah* and he will not ask of people."[20] Perhaps Allāh mentioned this group separately due to the fact that they are generally not known and deserve particular attention.

---

[19] *Sūrah at-Tawbah,* 9:60.
[20] Al-Bukhārī and Muslim.

Zakāh to Relatives

Among the poor and needy, those with the most right to one's *zakāh* are his Muslim relatives with the exception of parents, grandparents, children and grandchildren. It is prohibited to give to ascendants and descendants as well as to one's wife. The reason is that when any of these close family members is in need, it becomes the legal responsibility of a Muslim to take care of them within his means. According to the *sharī'ah,* anyone who would be the legal heir of a relative if he was rich is bound by law to take care of him when he is poor. *Zakāh* may not be given to one's dependants, but it earns additional reward when given to other needy relatives such as brothers, uncles or cousins. The Messenger of Allāh (ﷺ) said, "*Ṣadaqah* to a needy person is a *ṣadaqah,* but to a relative it is a *ṣadaqah* and a bond of kinship."[21] Scholars differ over the permissibility of a wife giving to her husband when he qualifies for *zakāh.*

It is <u>not</u> permitted to give poor and needy non-Muslims, even relatives, from *zakāh,* although they may be given from one's voluntary *ṣadaqah.* Again, this is based on the *ḥadīth* stating that it is "to be taken from their rich and given to their poor," the pronoun "their" referring to Muslims.

Preference

Although theoretically *zakāh* can be given to any Muslim who qualifies, scholars prefer that it be given to those who practice their religion conscientiously and do not commit major sins. It is disliked (*makrūh*) to give to those who do not pray, for example, and it is prohibited to give it with the knowledge that the recipient will waste or use it for something unlawful. However, when it is expected that the *zakāh* will help a person to reform or encourage him to become righteous, it may be given to him.

Ability to Work

A man who is healthy and able to earn a living has no right to *zakāh.* One cannot judge merely by appearance, however, for there could be other factors involved, such as a lack of job opportunities. During the Farewell Ḥajj while Allāh's Messenger (ﷺ) was distributing *ṣadaqah,* two men approached and requested a portion. He looked at them and saw that they were sturdy, so he said, "If you wish, I will give you, but there is no share for a rich man nor for one who is strong and able to earn."[22] Those who refuse to work out of laziness or preferring to spend their time in voluntary worship should not be encouraged to do so and may not be given *zakāh.*

---

[21] Aḥmad, at-Tirmidhī and an-Nasā'ī – *ṣaḥeeḥ.*
[22] Aḥmad, Abū Dāwūd and an-Nasā'ī – *ṣaḥeeḥ.*

Many contemporary scholars have ruled that education may be considered to be among the basic needs in modern society, especially in the case of students who will eventually use their knowledge as a means of support for themselves and their families. It can thus be compared to tools of trade; hence, *zakāh* can be given to assist poor and needy students to complete their studies on the condition that the chosen field is an Islāmically lawful one.

Amount to Be Given

Among the purposes of *zakāh* is to eliminate need and make the poor self-sufficient. Therefore, whenever possible, enough should be given to each recipient to provide him with a permanent solution. It could, in fact, be preferable to solve the problem of one person or family than to help several for a limited period. 'Umar bin al-Khaṭṭāb said, "When you give, give enough [to relieve poverty]."

A poor person is allowed to accept and request *zakāh* only as long as his condition lasts. Qubayṣah bin Mukhāriq had taken on a debt for someone and sought aid from the Prophet (ﷺ), who asked him to wait until some *ṣadaqah* was sent to him. Then he (ﷺ) said, "O Qubayṣah, asking is not permitted except for three: a man who is responsible for another's debt until he settles it – then he must stop, and a man who was struck by a calamity so his property was destroyed until he again becomes self-sufficient, and a man afflicted by poverty when three mentally sound members of his people testify to it, until he becomes self-sufficient. But any other requests, O Qubayṣah, are unlawful and are taken unlawfully."[23]

3. Zakāh Employees (العاملين عليها)

These are the collectors of *zakāh*, guards and distributors employed full-time by an Islāmic state, whose salaries are paid from *zakāh* funds. These employees should be Muslims, but poverty is not a condition since their share is a salary in payment for a service and not a means of aid or assistance. The wages must be comparable to those for other government jobs and adequate to maintain the employee and his family. In the present day the gathering and distribution of *zakāh* is dependant upon individuals and organizations rather than state employed collectors, and is ultimately the responsibility of every owner of wealth.

4. Those Who Integrate Hearts (المؤلفة قلوبهم)

The recipients in this category are those whose support is sought and expected or those who can influence others for the benefit of Islām. It is the

---

[23] Aḥmad and Muslim.

only category in which there is the possibility of granting a portion to non-Muslims, although scholars allow this only in cases of explicit need. This type of *zakāh* may be given to the following:

* Muslim leaders who can influence non-Muslim associates to accept Islām
* Muslim leaders of weak faith and resolve but who are obeyed among their people, in order to strengthen their commitment to Islām
* Muslims in positions of danger from enemies or near the frontlines, for defense
* Non-Muslims who are expected to embrace Islām with material encouragement
* Non-Muslims who would otherwise be a threat, in order to protect defenseless Muslims from attack, aggression or other harm

5. To Free Captives (في الرقاب)

Captives include prisoners of war, those imprisoned unjustly, and slaves, and again applies to Muslims. It is not permissible to allow Muslim prisoners to remain in enemy hands when it is possible to ransom them, and *zakāh* funds may be used for this purpose. They may also be used to buy a Muslim slave in order to set him/her free, or to help one purchase his own freedom according to an agreement with the owner. When asked about a deed that would draw one close to Paradise and distance him from Hellfire, the Prophet (ﷺ) replied, "Free a person and release a neck from bondage."[24]

6. Those with Insurmountable Debt (الغارمين)

These are people burdened with debts impossible for them to pay, even in the long term. They are of two kinds:

* Debtors in extreme poverty whose debts have accumulated or those who owe due to an emergency that compelled them to borrow or defer payment of bills.
* Persons who take upon themselves the debt of another or serve as a guarantor. (Refer to the *ḥadīth* of Qubayṣah above.) They may collect *zakāh* and *ṣadaqah* in order to relieve the debt, and this is the traditional practice for payments of *diyah* (blood money), which are usually beyond the means of an individual. There is no stipulation of the guarantor's inability to fulfill the debt himself, and he is not obligated to do so.

7. For the Cause of Allāh (في سبيل الله)

Literally, "in the way of Allāh," it means the way to His acceptance and approval through knowledge and deeds. The majority of scholars have

---

[24]Aḥmad – *ḥasan.*

interpreted it to mean, primarily, *jihād* in the form of armed struggle, and that *zakāh* can be given to volunteers among the *mujāhideen* but not those soldiers who receive a salary from the government. It is of no matter whether they are rich or poor. The Prophet (ﷺ) said, "*Ṣadaqah* is not permitted to the rich except for five: the fighter in the way of Allāh, its collector [for distribution], the bearer of [another's] debt, a man who purchased it with his own wealth, and one who gave it to a poor neighbor, who in turn gave him something of it as a gift."[25]

Zakāh may also be given as a contribution to the war effort for *jihād* and for defense when state funds are inadequate – for weapons and arms, for equipment, transport and food for soldiers, for the establishment of military hospitals, etc. There is a particular condition attached to *zakāh* used for this purpose: that whatever is purchased with it and is still intact or can be utilized once the war is over must be returned to the state treasury (*bayt al-māl*) and does not become the property of soldiers or officers.

A second concept included in this category is *da'wah* (propagation). It has become increasingly important in modern times to educate and train *da'wah* workers and to send them out to judiciously invite people to Islam. Those *imāms,* teachers and aid workers residing temporarily or permanently in non-Muslim countries must be supported through *zakāh* and *ṣadaqah* when *da'wah* activities consume the time they would otherwise have used for earning a living. The same applies to students preparing for this kind of work, even while doing so within Islāmic environments.

Zakāh may be given in countries where Muslims are a minority for the building and establishment of Islāmic schools, *masjids* and other centers of religious education and aid for Muslims and *da'wah* to non-Muslims. It can be used for the salaries of teachers in those schools or centers unless they happen to be well to do, in which case it is disliked (*makrūh*) to accept payment for religious knowledge. It is not permissible, however, to use *zakāh* for such purposes within Muslim countries, and only voluntary *ṣadaqah* is acceptable therein for the construction of *masjids,* schools, hospitals, etc., which is actually the responsibility of their governments.

Most scholars do not consider sending someone to *hajj* as part of this category, as a person without the financial means is not under obligation to perform *hajj.* In the Qur'ān, Allāh has stipulated that it is for **"whoever is able to find thereto a way."** (3:97) Since financial inability exempts one from this duty, *zakāh* should be spent on more urgent matters.

8. The Traveler (ابن السبيل)

All scholars have agreed that a traveler who is stranded with insufficient funds to enable him to return home (perhaps due to loss or theft) may be given

---

[25]Aḥmad, Abū Dāwūd and Ibn Mājah – *ṣaheeḥ.*

from *zakāh* even though he might posses wealth in his place of origin. Some stipulate that this is only in case he is unable to find anyone who will lend him the means of return. Eligibility in this category is due to the temporary condition of poverty.

Choice of Categories and Priority

The aforementioned eight categories were specified by Allāh as lawful recipients of *zakāh,* but it is not necessary, or usually even possible, to give to each of them equally, nor is it preferred. Some of them may be given more than others according to need, or a Muslim may confine himself to one category alone. It is preferable, whenever possible, to fulfill a particular need or solve a problem completely when funds are sufficient for that, and a single case of urgency might consume one's entire payment. Priorities are therefore left to the discretion of the owners and distributors of *zakāh.*

Unlawful Recipients and Error in Distribution

Allāh has limited the recipients of *zakāh* to the eight categories that have been defined, and it is not permitted to any others. Specifically, it is prohibited for the following:

- The rich and self-sufficient
- Non-Muslims, excepting those mentioned under "Integration of Hearts" (category no. 4)
- Banū Hāshim, the family of the Prophet (ﷺ), as mentioned by him in *ḥadīths* narrated by al-Bukhārī and Muslim
- Dependants among family members, in particular the wife, parents and children, for whom a Muslim is responsible by law
- Those who refuse to work although they have the ability
- Use for government projects, official state functions, the construction of schools, hospitals, roads, *masjids,* etc., within Muslim countries
- Funerals, shrouds, weddings, celebrations, accommodation for guests and the like; in short, anything outside of the eight designated categories

If a Muslim should make a mistake in the payment of his *zakāh* and later learns that it went to a non-eligible recipient, most scholars consider that the debt remains and that the obligation must still be fulfilled by delivering the *zakāh* to its rightful place, even if it means giving it once again.

$$\text{﴿إِنَّ اللَّهَ يَأْمُرُكُمْ أَن تُؤَدُّوا الْأَمَانَاتِ إِلَى أَهْلِهَا﴾}$$

"Indeed, Allāh commands you to render trusts to whom they are due."[26]

---

[26]*Sūrah an-Nisā',* 4:58.

Although generally it is preferred to conceal *ṣadaqah,* especially the voluntary type (refer to 2:271), it can also be beneficial to let people know about the fulfillment of one's Islāmic obligations to encourage others to do the same. And a person who is reluctant to accept aid might be encouraged by the knowledge that it is his right. On the other hand, someone else might accept it more readily if told it was an anonymous gift. Therefore, it is permissible to mention that what is given is *zakāh,* just as it is permissible not to, and the matter may be left to the judgement of those who know the recipient and his circumstances.

ṢADAQAT AL-FIṬR

Ṣadaqat al-fiṭr is also known as *zakāt al-fiṭr,* perhaps owing to its obligatory nature. "*Fiṭr*" refers to the cessation of Ramadhān fasting, which is when it is due. It is not to be confused with the *zakāh* of wealth (*zakāt al-māl*) previously outlined, and its rulings differ.

According to authentic *ḥadīths, ṣadaqat al-fiṭr* is due at the end of Ramadhān and before the *'Eid* prayer on each Muslim (irrespective of age) in households possessing sufficient food to last 24 hours. Ibn 'Umar reported: "The Messenger of Allāh (ﷺ) made obligatory *zakāt al-fiṭr* at the end of Ramadhān – a measure of dates or barley – for the slave and the freeman, the male and the female, and the young and the old among the Muslims."[27] Its purpose is to purify people from any minor sins or improper behavior they might have committed inadvertently while fasting and to enable the poor to enjoy their *'Eid* without having to work or search for food. It is a religious obligation for the head of every Muslim family to give on behalf of his dependants and the residents of his household, including servants and permanent guests. A baby born any time before the *'Eid* prayer should be counted as a member of the household, while a person who died before then need not be included.

Ṣadaqat al-fiṭr becomes obligatory at sunset of the final day of Ramadhān, although it may be given a few days earlier. But it must be distributed by the morning of *'Eid al-Fiṭr* before the people go out for the *'Eid* prayer. It is not permissible to delay beyond its due time unless one is prevented by circumstances beyond his control, in which case it remains a debt until cleared.

Recipients are the same ones listed under the eight categories designated for *zakāh* of wealth, although the poor and needy have the greatest right to *ṣadaqat al-fiṭr.*

The traditional practice mentioned in the *sunnah* has been to give a measure of staple food on behalf of each member of a household. Abū Sa'eed

---

[27]Al-Bukhārī and Muslim.

al-Khudrī said, "During the time of the Prophet (ﷺ), on the Day of *Fiṭr,* we used to give out one measure [*sā'*] of food, and our food was barley, raisins, dried cheese and dates."[28] This measure is the equivalent of approximately 2.5 to 3 kilograms, and similar staples such as rice, wheat and corn have also been included. The Ḥanafī school of thought allows that the price of that portion may be given instead, and an increasing number of scholars are subscribing to this view in modern times.

FURTHER OBLIGATIONS PERTAINING TO WEALTH

The system of *zakāh* ordained by Allāh, the Exalted, is the ideal way to meet the needs of poorer sectors of society without causing hardship to the rich. History bears witness to the fact that at times when Muslims conscientiously observed Allāh's right to a small portion of the wealth He bestows upon His servants, poverty among them was completely eliminated. Destitution among Muslims today is the direct outcome of disobedience and negligence by a large number of the wealthiest members of the *ummah* and their disregard of basic duties and obligations. 'Alī bin Abī Ṭālib said, "Indeed, Allāh imposed on the rich from their properties an amount sufficient for the poor. So if they go hungry or unclothed or suffer hardship, it is because of what the rich withhold, and Allāh will have the right to call them [the latter] to account on the Day of Resurrection and punish them for it." Scholars agree that when the *zakāh* distributed is insufficient to cover basic necessities for the poor or when Muslims are struck by calamities, there is a further obligation upon the community, which is limited only by relief of the affliction. An Islāmic state is then authorized to tax the wealthy accordingly.

Therefore, anyone who finds a Muslim in urgent need must help according to his ability without regard to *niṣāb* or the passing of a year, and his contribution will be amply rewarded by Allāh as an act of worship. Evidence for this is in His commands:

﴿وَآتِ ذَا الْقُرْبَى حَقَّهُ وَالْمِسْكِينَ وَابْنَ السَّبِيلِ﴾

"And give the relative his right, and the needy and the traveler."[29]

﴿وَاعْبُدُوا اللَّهَ وَلَا تُشْرِكُوا بِهِ شَيْئًا وَبِالْوَالِدَيْنِ إِحْسَانًا وَبِذِي الْقُرْبَى وَالْيَتَامَى وَالْمَسَاكِينِ وَالْجَارِ ذِي الْقُرْبَى وَالْجَارِ الْجُنُبِ وَالصَّاحِبِ بِالْجَنْبِ وَابْنِ السَّبِيلِ وَمَا مَلَكَتْ أَيْمَانُكُمْ﴾

"Worship Allāh and associate nothing with Him, and to parents [show] good treatment, and to relatives, orphans, the needy, the near neighbor, the neighbor farther away, the companion at your side, the traveler, and those whom your right hands possess."[30]

---

[28]Al-Bukhārī.

[29]*Sūrah al-Isrā',* 17:26.

[30]*Sūrah an-Nisā',* 4:36.

All of them have rights over a Muslim that cannot be ignored, and even more so when they are in need. The Prophet (ﷺ) warned, "He who shows not mercy to the people will not be shown mercy by Allāh."[31] And he (ﷺ) said, "A Muslim is the brother of a Muslim; he neither wrongs nor betrays him."[32] Anyone who leaves another destitute while able to assist him has surely betrayed him.

In the Qur'ān, Allāh addressed inquiries by the *ṣaḥābah*:

﴿وَيَسْأَلُونَكَ مَاذَا يُنفِقُونَ قُلِ الْعَفْوَ﴾

"And they ask you [O Muḥammad] what they should spend. Say, 'The excess.'"[33]

And Allāh's Messenger (ﷺ) once ordered, "Let whoever has an extra mount give it to one who has none, and let whoever has extra supplies give to one who has none." Abū Saʿeed al-Khudrī added, "He went on to mention so many kinds of possessions that we thought no one of us had the right to any surplus."[34]

It was a consensus among the *ṣaḥābah* and their students that there is indeed a right from property other than *zakāh*. Moreover, a Muslim is not permitted to eat a dead animal or pig flesh as long as there is food available with others because it is their duty to feed the hungry. He even has the right to fight for it (see 49:9), and if the withholder should be killed, the hungry person is exempted from punishment under the law.

VOLUNTARY ṢADAQAH

﴿مَن ذَا الَّذِي يُقْرِضُ اللَّهَ قَرْضًا حَسَنًا فَيُضَاعِفَهُ لَهُ وَلَهُ أَجْرٌ كَرِيمٌ﴾

"Who is it that would loan Allāh a goodly loan so He will multiply it for him and he will have a noble reward?"[35]

The Qur'ān and *sunnah* emphatically encourage the expenditure of both wealth and effort in the way of Allāh as a means to His approval and reward. Allāh said:

﴿آمِنُوا بِاللَّهِ وَرَسُولِهِ وَأَنفِقُوا مِمَّا جَعَلَكُم مُّسْتَخْلَفِينَ فِيهِ فَالَّذِينَ آمَنُوا مِنكُمْ وَأَنفَقُوا لَهُمْ أَجْرٌ كَبِيرٌ﴾

"Believe in Allāh and His Messenger and spend from that for which He made you responsible. For those who have believed among you and spent, there will be a great reward."[36]

---

[31] Al-Bukhārī and Muslim.

[32] Al-Bukhārī and Muslim.

[33] *Sūrah al-Baqarah,* 2:219.

[34] Muslim.

[35] *Sūrah al-Ḥadeed,* 57:11.

[36] *Sūrah al-Ḥadeed,* 57:7.

﴿لَن تَنَالُواْ ٱلْبِرَّ حَتَّىٰ تُنفِقُواْ مِمَّا تُحِبُّونَ ۚ وَمَا تُنفِقُواْ مِن شَيْءٍ فَإِنَّ ٱللَّهَ بِهِ عَلِيمٌ﴾

"Never will you attain righteousness until you spend from what you love. And whatever you spend – indeed, Allāh is Knowing of it."[37]

﴿مَّثَلُ ٱلَّذِينَ يُنفِقُونَ أَمْوَالَهُمْ فِي سَبِيلِ ٱللَّهِ كَمَثَلِ حَبَّةٍ أَنبَتَتْ سَبْعَ سَنَابِلَ فِي كُلِّ سُنبُلَةٍ مِّائَةُ حَبَّةٍ ۗ وَٱللَّهُ يُضَاعِفُ لِمَن يَشَاءُ ۚ وَٱللَّهُ وَاسِعٌ عَلِيمٌ﴾

"The example of those who spend their wealth in the way of Allāh is like a grain which grows seven spikes; in each spike is a hundred grains. And Allāh multiplies [the reward] for whom He wills. And Allāh is all-Encompassing and Knowing."[38]

And the Prophet (ﷺ) said, "He among you who can avoid the Fire – let him [do so] even with half a date, and if he finds none, then by a good word."[39] And, "No morning comes upon the people but that two angels descend, and one of them says, 'O Allāh, give one who spends [on others] replacement,' while the other says, 'O Allāh, give one who withholds ruin.'"[40]

The Nature of Sadaqah

The Messenger of Allāh (ﷺ) mentioned numerous forms of *ṣadaqah* in authentic *ḥadīths* as examples and illustrations, among them: charities from one's property, helping someone in distress, effecting a just settlement between two parties, lifting something for a weak person, directing the blind, helping the deaf to understand, visiting the ill, feeding the hungry, clothing the poor, removing harmful objects from the road, planting a seed or shoot, a kind word or smile, benevolence in the home, praising and glorifying Allāh, and even refraining from wrong. There is no limit, for the Prophet (ﷺ) confirmed on several occasions that "every good deed is a *ṣadaqah*."[41] And he said, "Whoever directs to something good will have the same reward as the one who does it."[42] This section, however, deals with material forms of *ṣadaqah*.

Recipients

Those eligible for voluntary *ṣadaqah* are not restricted to the categories of recipients for obligatory *zakāh*. However, anyone who aims to please Allāh thereby needs to choose judiciously.

---

[37] *Sūrah Āli 'Imrān*, 3:92.
[38] *Sūrah al-Baqarah*, 2:261.
[39] Aḥmad and Muslim.
[40] Muslim.
[41] Al-Bukhārī and Muslim.
[42] Muslim.

Those most deserving of one's *ṣadaqah* are his family members. The Prophet (ﷺ) said, "When one of you is poor, he should begin with himself; and if there is extra, his dependants; and if there is extra, his relatives; and if there is extra, then here and there."[43] And he warned, "It is sufficient sin for a person to neglect those for whom he is responsible."[44] He meant it is sufficient to place him in Hell. He also said, "The best *ṣadaqah* is to the blood relative who is hostile."[45]

Voluntary *ṣadaqah,* unlike *zakāh,* may be given to non-Muslims in need, especially relatives. The Prophet (ﷺ) told Asmā', whose mother was a polytheist, to aid her and keep the relationship.[46] On various occasions he (ﷺ) was generous to non-Muslims, including war captives.

It may also be used for the care of animals which would otherwise suffer due to neglect. Nonetheless, humankind should take priority, especially one's fellow Muslims.

A Wife's Sadaqah from Her Husband's Property

The wife may give *ṣadaqah* from her husband's house on the condition that she is certain of his approval. It is prohibited otherwise, except for small amounts of food that are given customarily. Asmā' mentioned to the Prophet (ﷺ) that she sometimes gave to poor people who came to her door without her husband's permission. He told her, "Give a small amount and do not withhold, or Allāh will withhold from you."[47] And 'Ā'ishah reported that he (ﷺ) said: "When a woman gives out something of the food in her house which is not spoiled, she will have the reward for what she gave and her husband will have the reward for what he obtained, and the caretaker will have the same. The reward of each will not lessen that of the others at all."[48]

The Continuing Sadaqah (Sadaqah Jāriyah)

The Messenger of Allāh (ﷺ) informed his *ummah*: "When a person dies, his deeds are ended except for three: a continuing *ṣadaqah* or knowledge by which benefit is derived or a righteous child who supplicates for him."[49] There are many kinds of *ṣadaqah* that continue after one's death, among the most common: the construction of a *masjid*, school or hospital, the excavation of a well, the planting of land for food, the establishment of a trust or scholarship,

---

[43] Aḥmad and Muslim.
[44] Muslim.
[45] Aḥmad – *ṣaheeḥ.*
[46] Al-Bukhārī.
[47] Al-Bukhārī and Muslim.
[48] Al-Bukhārī.
[49] Aḥmad and Muslim.

and the publication of beneficial knowledge – although the possibilities are unlimited. There are also many deeds with continuing benefit that require little financial means and only the correct intention, such as teaching a poor student, training a worker, or planting a single tree. As the Prophet (ﷺ) disclosed: "No Muslim plants a seedling or a crop from which a person, animal, bird or anything eats but that it is for him a *ṣadaqah*."[50]

Invalid Sadaqah

A Muslim seeking Allāh's approval and pleasure by giving *ṣadaqah* must avoid invalidating it and making it unacceptable to Him through any of the following:

- Earning, accepting and giving what is unlawful (*ḥarām*) – The Prophet (ﷺ) said, "Indeed, Allāh is pure and only accepts what is pure."[51]

- Showing off or seeking a worldly benefit, praise or recognition for his gift – A *ḥadīth* narrated by Muslim states that a person who does so will stand before Allāh on the Day of Resurrection and be told, "You spent to be called generous, and it was said." Then he will be dragged into the Fire. And the Qur'ān warns:

$$﴿وَاعلَمُوا أَنَّ اللهَ يَعلَمُ مَا فِي أَنفُسِكُم فَاحذَرُوهُ﴾$$

"And know that Allāh knows what is within yourselves, so beware of Him."[52]

- Harming the recipient by either belittling him, making him feel indebted, speaking of the *ṣadaqah* in front of others, or expecting from him a favor in return. Allāh said:

$$﴿يَا أَيُّهَا الَّذِينَ آمَنُوا لاَ تُبطِلُوا صَدَقَاتِكُم بِالــمَنِّ وَالأَذَى كَالَّذِي يُنفِقُ مَالَهُ رِئَاءَ النَّاسِ وَلاَ يُؤمِنُ بِالله وَاليَومِ الآخِرِ﴾$$

"O you who have believed, do not invalidate your charities with reminders [of it] or injury as does one who spends his wealth to be seen by the people and does not believe in Allāh and the Last Day."[53]

SHOWING APPRECIATION FOR ZAKĀH AND ṢADAQAH

It was the practice of the Prophet (ﷺ) to supplicate for those who gave *zakāh* and *ṣadaqah* and ask Allāh to bless them and their wealth in compliance with Allāh's words:

---

[50]Al-Bukhārī.
[51]Muslim.
[52]*Sūrah al-Baqarah*, 2:235.
[53]*Sūrah al-Baqarah*, 2:264.

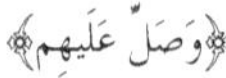

"And invoke blessings upon them."[54]

And he (ﷺ) instructed, "Whoever does for you a good deed, reward him. But if you find nothing, then supplicate for him until you know you have rewarded him."[55]

Thus, is it also a *sunnah* practice for the *imām* or anyone else who collects *zakāh* or *ṣadaqah* for others to do the same. They used to say, "May Allāh reward you for what you have given and grant you blessing in what you have kept." Allāh's Messenger (ﷺ) said, "Anyone to whom some good was done and said to the one who did it, '*Jazāk-Allāhu khayran*' ['May Allāh reward you with good.'] has accorded him the utmost appreciation."[56] That is because Allāh, the Exalted, will give him the best compensation.

والحمد لله رب العالمين

---

[54]*Sūrah at-Tawbah,* 9:103.

[55]Aḥmad, Abū Dāwūd and an-Nasā'ī – *ṣaheeh.*

[56]At-Tirmidhī – *ṣaheeh.*

REFERENCES

Makki, Majd Aḥmad, *Fatāwā Muṣṭafa az-Zarqā,* Damascus: Dār al-Qalam, 1999.

al-Qaradawi, Yūsuf, *Fiqh az-Zakāh,* Cairo: 16th printing, 1985. (www.qaradawi.net)

Sabiq, as-Sayyid, *Fiqh as-Sunnah,* Cairo: Dār al-Fatḥ lil-I'lām al-'Arabī, 11th edition, 1994.